Kiseto and
Setoguro

FAMOUS CERAMICS OF JAPAN 10

Kiseto and Setoguro

Shōsaku Furukawa

KODANSHA INTERNATIONAL LTD.
Tokyo, New York, San Francisco

Translated by N. Robert Huey

Distributed in the United States by Kodansha International/USA Ltd.,
through Harper & Row, Publishers, Inc., 10 East 53rd Street, New
York, New York 10022.

Published by Kodansha International Ltd., 12–21 Otowa 2-chome,
Bunkyo-ku, Tokyo 112 and Kodansha International/USA Ltd., 10
East 53rd Street, New York, New York 10022 and 44 Montgomery
Street, San Francisco, California 94104.

LCC 82–48782
ISBN 0–87011–567–7
ISBN 4–7700–1058–3 (in Japan)

Library of Congress Cataloging in Publication Data

Furukawa, Shōsaku, 1911–
　Kiseto and Setoguro.

　(Famous ceramics of Japan; 10)
　Translation of: Kiseto Setoguro.
　1. Pottery, Japanese—Japan—Gifu-ken.　2. Seto
pottery. I. Title. II. Series.
N4168.G5F87 1983　　　738.3′7　　　82–48782
ISBN 0–87011-567-7 (Kodansha International/USA)

Kiseto and Setoguro Wares

About a forty-minute train ride from Nagoya on the Chūō Line brings one to Tajimi. The area around here and the town of Toki, which lies to the east, is known as Higashi Mino and has long been a pottery region. Many different kinds of pottery have been made here over the years.

Particularly in the Momoyama period (1573–1615), this area produced a variety of beautiful pottery styles that can only be called the crystallization of the spirit and skill of the Japanese: white Shino ware, its materials soft like a light snowfall; Oribe, with its peculiar shapes, lively designs, and characteristic vivid green color; Kiseto ware, with its refined, yellow surface; and the jet-black Setoguro. Yellow, black, white, and green—to these colors were applied various creative techniques and a keen aesthetic sense, and the pottery of Mino came to fruition during the Momoyama period, one of the most vigorous eras in Japan's cultural history.

Among these types of pottery, Kiseto and Setoguro do not seem to be as widely known as Shino and Oribe. Perhaps one of the reasons for this is that there are far fewer extant examples of these Seto types. Some superb pieces of Kiseto and Setoguro ware remain from the brief period of 1573–96 (the Tenshō and Bunroku eras), but little else is known about the two types of pottery, which disappeared from the scene shortly after that. In this book, the reader can only be shown a mere impression of this fascinating pottery, yet it is my pleasure if this helps the reader toward a deeper appreciation when he or she, sometime in the future, has a chance to see the actual pieces themselves.

"There's no flower that does not begin with a bud." So, too, with Kiseto and Setoguro. The iron and pale yellow glazes of Koseto (Old Seto) ware, which had been produced at Seto and Mino during the Kamakura (1185–1333) and Muromachi (1333–1573) periods, became associated with the *wabi* tea ceremony style, and a new pottery blossomed forth.

In both the earlier and later Seto ware, a kind of medieval sense of propriety prevailed, and from the middle of the Tenshō era (1573–92) on through the Bunroku era (1592–96), some excellent pieces were made.

Although Kiseto serving dishes were often used as teabowls (see Plates 22–27), there is only one example of a Kiseto piece made specifically as a teabowl—the bowl known as *Asaina*. But the most commonly found Kiseto pieces are the banded *dōhimo* and *dōjime* serving dishes with simple lips, the gong-shaped *rinka* (scalloped) bowls, the hour-glass-shaped flower vases, a tapered, jewel-shaped incense box, a hexagonal saké cup, and so on. Often these pieces have a short foot and a gently curved base, like a go-stone box. These are the representative shapes of Kiseto ware.

On the other hand, teabowls were about the only kind of Setoguro made. In other words, one might say that, in the formal tea ceremony, Kiseto ware was used mostly for the meal service, while Setoguro was chosen for its teabowls. Judging from the scarcity of the pieces, and their formal shapes, they must have been used only by the upper classes. With its delicate, gentle color, and the light sensation imparted to one's hands by its thin-walled construction, Kiseto is somehow feminine. As for Setoguro teabowls, their jet black glaze, which was originally a result of their having been used to check kiln temperatures, led them to become highly prized for use in the *wabi* style tea ceremony favored by Sen no Rikyū. The feeling they impart is strictly masculine. In their time, these pieces were cherished by Kyoto people of breeding and refined taste. (The use of Setoguro in determining kiln temperature is discussed below.)

It is said that the best Kiseto was fired at the Kamashita kilns of Ōgaya, and the best Setoguro at the Sengen kilns. But such superb pots did not just abruptly come into being. The forerunners of Kiseto and Setoguro were fired at kilns that preceded these.

And in the same way, Shino and Oribe wares, so representative of the Momoyama period, came into being as a result of the search for a beauty beyond that of Kiseto and Setoguro.

Momoyama pottery in the Mino area was born when local potters' groups amalgamated with warrior-led potter's guilds from Owari Province (modern Gifu and Aichi prefectures), with Korean potters who came to Mino from the north by way of Echizen (present-day Fukui Prefecture), and with professional literati from Kyoto, who specialized in painting. These groups combined in lively interchange and produced some of Japan's greatest pottery.

It is sometimes said that Setoguro copies the black Korean ware known in Japan as *Kurokōrai* and that Kiseto reflects the three-color glazed ware of Tang dynasty China. But Setoguro's jet black is incomparable, owing to its being pulled out of the firing early to check the kiln's temperature. And Kiseto's yellow and green developed from a new-found technique of firing at high temperatures. One cannot help but wonder why these two types of pottery disappeared so quickly.

Even in the midst of the violent warfare being waged to establish a new social order in the sixteenth century, the generals found time for the tea ceremony; tea masters and artisans and urban merchants —all these people had their connections with Mino.

The rise and fall of the kilns at Mino, where Kiseto and Setoguro gave birth to Shino and Oribe ware, provides an interesting view into human history through the records left by pottery.

KILNS WHERE KISETO WAS FIRED

The Kamashita Kiln at Ōgaya

Tōkurō Katō, in his book *Kiseto* published in 1933 wrote that Kiseto ware was conceived at the Sobokai kiln (also known as the Sengen kiln), achieved its fullest development at the Kamashita kiln, then afterwards spread to the Mutabora, Naka, and Ōhira kilns before completely disappearing.

In 1932, under Mr. Katō's direction, an orderly and systematic excavation in the Mino area was carried out for the first time at the site of the Kamashita kiln. Kiseto shards bearing the date Bunroku 2 (1593) were unearthed and played an important role in dating the Mino kilns. However, the bulk of the evidence has been destroyed by the ravages of war.

Many of the Kiseto pieces from this kiln are small undecorated dishes covered with a shiny glaze. The hexagonal saké cups found among these pots gave rise to the term "saké cup type" (*guinomi-de*) Kiseto ware to describe this style.

Also fired at this kiln were bowls, serving dishes, plates, and incense burners. These are characterized by thin walls and soft glazing, stamped chrysanthemum or paulownia designs, and incised motifs such as plum blossom, young spring grasses, iris, dayflower, giant radish, turnip, chrysanthemums, or autumn grasses. Onto these designs, a fresh copper-green or black iron glaze was splashed. The results are marvelous. Among these pieces is a large, scalloped (*rinka*) bowl etched with an iris design. The

A "hole kiln" (*anagama*) site, Kamakura and Muromachi periods

Site of a partially underground kiln, where Kiseto, Setoguro, and Shino wares were fired in the Momoyama period

A "split-bamboo" style kiln, Momoyama and Edo periods

glaze texture is quiet and soft and resembles fried bean curd. The glazing on this large bowl, representative of one kind of Kiseto glaze, is called the "iris type" or "fried bean curd type."

In the vicinity of Ōgaya can be found the special kind of iron-rich red clay that is indispensible for producing Kiseto's soft color. This clay is also responsible for the accidental—but prized—burn marks found on the inside of the foot of some Kiseto pieces and for the dark rust color found in Shino ware. This red clay was sometimes used for circular fireclay pads, and the story is well known in Japanese pottery circles of how Toyozō Arakawa discovered in Mino (not in Seto, where Shino was once thought to have originated) the remains of the Momoyama tea pottery kiln site where Shino ware was first made. He made his discovery by following up on his observation that bits of this red clay had been burnt into the inside of the foot of a Shino teabowl he had seen.

The saggars used at Ōgaya were also of this iron-rich, refractory clay. Other kilns such as Ōhira and Motoyashiki also used saggars made of clay that comes from their surrounding areas. Since each of these clays has its own peculiarities, it is usually possible to tell from looking at a saggar of that time which kiln site it came from.

The Kamashita kiln was still a primitive, simple structure, large, and partially above ground, and it was not very efficient. It must have taken a great deal of hard work and manpower to fire it. In the hottest part of the kiln, next to the fire, where reduction takes place, the potters placed the Shino pieces, with their thick, basic feldspathic glaze. Behind these, yet still in a fairly hot part of the kiln, were placed the "saké cup type" Kiseto pieces, with their ash and feldspathic glaze. Toward the rear of the kiln, where the temperature is not so high and oxidation occurs, were placed the "iris type" Kiseto pieces, covered with a thin ash glaze to which red or some such iron-rich clay had been added. In the bottom of Kiseto pieces, small rocks, or rocks wedged in by bochi fireclay pads were placed, and inside the foot, a thin, round fireclay pad. In Shino pieces, "pin" fireclay pads or thick, round pads were used. These pads are evidence of the care taken to prevent fusion when both Kiseto, with its thin, highly liquid ash glaze, and Shino, with its thick, viscous glaze, which required high temperatures, were fired in the same kiln.

In the case of the copper-green color, when it is fired at too high a temperature, the color fades, and in a reducing atmosphere it fires red. How did the potters avoid such color change? What pains they must have taken to learn the optimal firing conditions!

Art historians and collectors in Japan are apt to shine a spotlight on the people who commissioned and used these works of pottery (that is, tea masters such as Sen no Rikyū or Furuta Oribe). But with many works of art, much is missed if we do not understand and take into consideration the potter who made the work. Looking into the actual process of how a work is created is just as important as studying the work itself.

The Motoyashiki kiln site at Ōgaya, Momoyama and Edo periods. Oribe ware mainly was fired here.

Coal was once used as fuel in Tajimi.

Contemporary kiln in Tajimi

The Ōhira, Naka, and Sengen Kiln Sites

Kiseto shards excavated from the Yoshiemon, Sei-dayu, and Yamanokami kiln sites at Ōhira reveal pottery of all types—plates, bowls, serving dishes, and so on. Some plates show stamped flower or grass designs and copper-green glaze. Others have incised giant radish, turnip, or plum blossom designs and again copper-green glaze. There are also rare plates on which pictures have been painted in under-glaze iron. And among the shards found at Ōhira, there are many *dōhimo* and *dōjime* serving dishes, comb-patterned bowls, *rinka* bowls, and pieces where underglaze iron has been applied to an incised design.

"Chrysanthemum plate type" Kiseto ware, representative of the Ōhira kilns and characterized by a foliate rim suggesting a chrysanthemum and generous application of copper green, came to be fired at Ōhira during the early and middle Edo period (1615–1868). Compared to other kilns, where Kiseto was made only for a short time, the Ōhira kilns continued production for a long period.

The distinctive feature of pieces from the Naka kilns is that although one or two simple flower or grass designs were stamped into their inside bottoms, these designs were not covered with copper green or iron. The fact that in pieces from the Naka kilns the characteristic Kiseto color is somewhat muddy is probably due to the red clay or to differences in the kilns themselves.

The Naka kiln site is located between the Ōgaya and Ōhira kilns, on the road that links the latter two. But in the days when these kilns were being fired, Ōhira was considered the center, and there was a road linking the Naka, Kamashita, and Mutabora kilns with the Sengen, Onada, and Amagane kilns.

The quality of the Kiseto ware excavated at the Sengen kiln site ranges from fine pieces with delicately incised grasses and flowers to coarse pots; from superb flower-stamped vessels, chrysanthemum plates, and gong-shaped bowls to work of a decidedly inferior nature.

For Kiseto ware, the works at the Takane kilns to the east of Ōhira, at Higashi no Mine, do not merit close examination, and the Motoyashiki kilns to the southwest hardly fired any Kiseto at all. As has been suggested, the fact that works from more distant kilns resemble the Ōhira pieces more than do those from nearby kilns seems to be because the style was carried from its source, the Mino potter Kagetoyo at Ōhira, by his workers or children setting up their own kilns.

Kilns along the Chūma Highway

Along the Chūma Highway, which ran from Owari to Iida, via Mino, can be found the Gōnoki, Ōkawa, Mizukami, Tanoso, and Mashizume kilns. Here a wide variety of *tenmoku* type teabowls were made—*tenmoku* teabowls with Kiseto glaze and copper-green markings; plain yellow *tenmoku* teabowls; white *tenmoku* teabowls; Shino *tenmoku* teabowls; Seto *tenmoku* teabowls; *tenmoku* teabowls covered with iron glaze on the inside and Shino glaze on the outside; and so on. The striking, large flat bowl seen in Plate 1, with its bold, fresh copper-green markings, stamped flower design, and comb pattern was also fired here. There are no other examples of such a powerful composition, in which four fireclay pad marks have been left behind on the inside bottom of the bowl. Severe, iron-glazed tea caddies, *natsume* tea caddies, Korean style saké bottles, "picture Shino" (*e-Shino*) small dishes, large dishes, and large bowls were also fired here. However, Setoguro was never made here, nor were Kiseto small serving dishes or Shino teabowls for the *wabi* type of tea ceremony.

In contrast to the older, Chinese-influenced style of tea ceremony, which used *tenmoku* bowls, the *wabi* style, perfected by Sen no Rikyū, later came to favor Oribe ware. One should be aware of the dif-

Dōjime shard unearthed at a kiln site at Ōhira

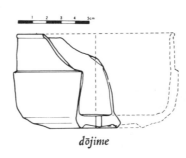

dōjime

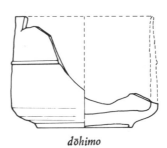

dōhimo

8

ference in time period between kilns that adhered to the tradition of firing only *tenmoku* style teabowls and those kilns that, even though they may in the beginning have made *tenmoku*, began to make the Kiseto, Setoguro, and Shino teabowls used in the *wabi* style tea ceremony. It is thought that since the kilns on the Chūma Highway were established about the same time as those at Ōgaya and had been around since before the great flowering of Mino pottery in the Momoyama period, they must have undertaken the Kiseto and Shino processes at an early date.

According to the *Ōhira Setogama yuisho* ("The History of the Seto Kilns at Ōhira"), the kiln-founder Kagetoyo's third son, San'emon, left the kiln of his eldest brother, Shin'emon, at Ōhira and went to the Mizukami kiln to make pottery. Even if we cannot be sure of the actual people involved, the pots and shards that remain fill in the story in detail.

Kiseto Glaze

In ancient times, when pots were fired in *anagama* ("hole kilns"), ash from the large quantities of wood fuel used melted onto the surface of a pot. From the *Engi shiki* ("Regulations of the Engi Era"; 927), we know that pottery thinly glazed with an ash and mud mixture was supplied from Owari (modern-day Gifu and Aichi prefectures) and Nagato (present-day Yamaguchi Prefecture) provinces for exclusive use by the imperial court. This is the earliest manifestation of Kiseto ware and is known as *Shino-utsuwa* type Kiseto.

From the Kamakura through the Muromachi periods, thick glazes made from ash to which feldspar had been added were made at the Konagaso kiln at Seto and at such Mino sites as the Anakōbō and Hinata kilns. And for the first time, saggars began to be used. At Mino, it appears that Old Seto yellow-glazed shallow teabowls, long-necked saké bottles, and Buddhist altar vases were fired together with Old Seto iron-glazed *tenmoku* teabowls. The use of ash glaze as the basic glaze for high-temperature firing is a specialty of Asian pottery.

It has been said that Shino and Kiseto came into being when potters tried to capture the effect of Chinese and Korean white and celadon porcelains. These Japanese potters, using pottery clay instead of porcelain, employed reduction firing to produce Shino in emulation of white porcelain and made Kiseto in the manner of celadon porcelain. In the case of Kiseto, oxidation firing causes iron in the ash glaze to fire a pale yellow color; with a reduction firing, a celadon color results.

Kiseto evolved from the early *Shino-utsuwa* type, to the "saké cup" and "iris" types of the Momoyama period, and on to the "chrysanthemum plate" type in the Edo period.

Setoguro, Shino, and Oribe, which went into a long decline after the Momoyama period, are presently being skillfully revived. As for Kiseto, for a while it looked as though some truly outstanding works might be produced, but it seems that in these modern times, that warm, faint color of Kiseto made in the Momoyama period has turned out to be difficult to reproduce.

With the radical changes that have taken place in our life-style, whether in a modern city or a mountain farming village, the potter has become estranged from firewood and charcoal. The kilns now burn mainly gas, oil, and electricity, and it has even become impossible to obtain high-quality wood ash, which used to be so readily available. "Kiseto owes everything to ash" is a common observation of ceramic historians, often accompanied by a description of the painstaking process required to produce

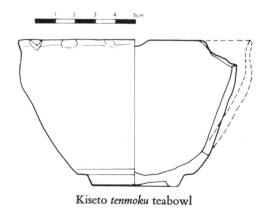

Kiseto *tenmoku* teabowl

the ash. But now, they say, the hardwood ash suitable for Kiseto is no longer obtainable. On the other hand, much good Shino ware has been produced recently by returning to the primitive *anagama* ("hole kiln") and relying on naturally occurring raw materials, such as feldspar and *oni-ita*, a kind of red clay deposit high in iron and manganese.

Setoguro, which derives its special quality solely from its having been pulled out of a white-hot kiln as test pieces, nowadays is fired by the easier and more reliable method of stacking it in saggars inside the kiln. Because the shapes are like Setoguro shapes and because it is black, people call it Setoguro. Today, what can possibly be passed on of the essence of both Kiseto and Setoguro?

From Kiln Test Pieces to Setoguro

Kiln test pieces were pieces of pottery removed from the kiln at some point in the firing to find out how the glaze was behaving and to check the temperature inside the kiln. An iron-glazed test piece turns black when it is suddenly removed from a white-hot kiln. In this dramatic transformation, the potters discovered beauty, and the birth of Setoguro was made possible. It was a splendid fusion of the Momoyama potters' enthusiasm for producing new things and the refined aesthetic sense of the *wabi* style tea masters.

A large number of Setoguro teabowl feet and partially fired teabowl shards have been excavated at kiln sites (see teabowl form sketches and Plates 50–52). This is proof that not just small tiles or fragments but rather whole teabowls were used as test pieces. One might think that a small piece would be sufficient for testing purposes, but in those days, when quite literally a potter's whole life went into the firing of the kiln, one can easily understand why he would choose the more cautious but certain way of checking the firing by using complete pots, for the slightest variation in temperature, weather conditions, wind speed, and so on, had direct influence on the success or failure of a firing. How much care those potters must have paid to the change of glaze characteristics in each small part of a test pot—the side facing the fire, the side away from the fire, the lip, the foot, the inside bottom. . . . And for this, how many Setoguro pieces were thrown out?

Furthermore, unlike Shino and Oribe ware, which were fired in saggars stacked on top of each other,

Setoguro ware was removed, one bowl at a time, through a small hole in the kiln. These test pieces were fired only in certain parts of the kiln, so naturally only a small number of pieces were made at one time; it seems likely that the limited number of test pieces might have been insufficient for a firing. It is not likely that many of the test pieces reached optimal glaze melting point to produce Setoguro black.

This, more than anything, must account for the fact that, while Setoguro teabowls were treated with the greatest of care by those in the world of tea, so few of them have been passed down to the present day. And the fact that, solely in the case of Setoguro, teabowls were the *only* shape to be fired indicates that these pots made the most appropriate test pieces.

An examination of some pieces that have been excavated from old kiln sites will shed more light on these points.

Shino glazed and Kiseto glazed test shards, pierced for easy removal from the kiln, along with pierced test pieces with black *tenmoku* glaze, have been excavated from the Ōkawa Higashi kiln site, along the Chūma Highway, where all types of *tenmoku* teabowls were fired. (It is thought that the reason completely formed teabowls had not been used as test pieces in ancient times was because there were no iron tools for pulling them out of the kiln.)

Seizō Hayashiya of the Tokyo National Museum has noted that the partially fired, low cylinder type teabowls that have been recovered from the Amagane kiln site, which had already stopped producing by the end of the Muromachi period, resemble the Raku teabowls made by Chōjirō, and he conjectures that these must mark the beginnings of the Setoguro style. Many teabowls of this (see Plate 31) and similar types have also been found at the Kamashita kiln site at Ōgaya and at other sites. The teabowl called *Fuyu no Yoru* ("Winter Night"; Plate 39) and the teabowl in Plate 35, both showing the marks created on Setoguro teabowls when they were pulled out of the kiln, are good examples of the color and shape that is seen in the later Raku ware.

Not a single, pierced test piece shard has been excavated from either the Sengen kiln, which made Kiseto ware and Setoguro teabowls, or the Kamashita kilns, where many famous Kiseto pieces were fired. Yet a number of fully formed test piece Setoguro teabowls have been unearthed there. And at the Ōhira kilns, *tenmoku* test pieces have been found.

From early on, *tenmoku*-glazed shards gave way to complete *tenmoku* teabowls for use as test pieces. Furthermore, starting below the lip, the body soon came to be rounded outward down to the hip so as to prevent slipping when the piece was removed from the kiln (Plates 31, 32). Then finally, low cylinder type teabowls, with low, small feet and horizontal bases, began to be made for use as test pieces. This became the basic shape for Setoguro teabowls (see teabowl shape sketches). At this stage, it is thought, the potters were striving for a flat-bottomed, stable saggar shape that could be safely pulled from the kiln without being dropped. Perhaps, then, one should think seriously about the theory that Shino teabowls evolved from the idea of a flat-based saggar with a foot attached. The Setoguro teabowls owned by the Fujita Art Museum have a shape somewhere between that of *tenmoku* teabowls and that of low cylinder type Setoguro teabowls, showing the Setogoro evolutionary process.

Setoguro teabowls took a great leap forward in the hands of tea masters, developing into a variety of forms, from quiet, dignified teabowls, to magnificent pieces for use in the *wabi* style tea ceremony. The basic low cylinder shape gave way to bowls on which tool and throwing marks were consciously emphasized. These bowls, with their gently formed lips and trimmed feet, were the forerunners of the very methodically formed Shino and Oribe teabowls. It is fascinating to see how the taste of the tea masters was gradually brought to bear on the Setoguro teabowl, elevating it from its original test-piece functionality to a personal, artistic form.

Setoguro Glaze

Once I was shown a jet-black glazed shard that had been excavated from the waste pile at the Sue ware kiln site on Mt. Inkyo. It was a piece that had been oxidized when fired in an *anagama* that was dug into a clay-bearing formation (*sabatsuchi*). Its surface was exactly like Setoguro.

It is suggested that the Setoguro glaze was perfected by gathering a large sampling of the various types of this *sabatsuchi* clay from the region of Kujiri, which were then fired to test their colors. This region was under the sea millions of years ago, and the *sabatsuchi* formation from here, which was built up by deposits of shells and materials from the ocean, contains salt from the sea water. The conditions are ideal for producing a vitrified black color from this clay's iron content.

The most beautiful Setoguro shards, which come from the Sengen kilns (Plate 51), are glazed with *oni-ita* clay, which has a high manganese content, so the surface is deeply lustrous. Along the Kukuri Highway, going from Tajimi toward Ōgaya, an abandoned mine can be seen. Manganese was mined here during the war for military purposes. At the point where this road comes out, below the Sengen kilns, the area was dug out just before the end of the war and an underground factory was built there to escape the bombing. The clays—*sabatsuchi* and *oni-ita*—are gifts of nature that allowed a jet-black beauty to be produced.

The story these silent shards have to tell is not to be recorded in words or pictures. Yet locked inside these pieces lies an understated record of events.

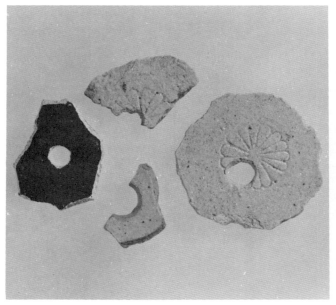

Pierced test pieces

Setoguro teabowl foot rings

THE PIONEERS OF MINO CERAMICS: FOREIGN BENEFACTORS

As stated earlier, the development of Mino pottery was due to the interaction of various influences in the Momoyama period, including local potters' groups and painters and tea masters from Kyoto.

One also must not forget the contributions of potters from Korea, who came to a foreign land—Japan—as a result of the Japanese invasions of their country in the 1590s, and brought new techniques with them.

In 1392 Korea's Koryŏ dynasty fell and was replaced by the Yi dynasty, which raised Confucianism to a state philosophy, persecuted Buddhists, and instituted a strict class system. To what extent Korean potters came willingly or were brought back by various feudal lords involved in the invasion of the peninsula will perhaps never be settled. Potters' position in Korean society was very low; the evidence is increasing that many followed the retreating military forces back to Japan of their own will. They came mainly to Kyushu and the Japan Sea coast.

Though at length they settled down in Japan, life was not always easy for them. Many must have been forced to do the cruelest labor, having no other means of making a living. Yet amidst all this, the skills they brought with them from their native country were passed down through their children and grandchildren. Their hardships greatly contributed to the flowering of Japan's ceramic art.

At the end of the sixteenth century, the Ikkō uprising was sweeping through the Japan Sea coast region, and it is thought that the Korean potters from that area came to Mino via the Echizen Highway, along with the spread of the Ikkō sect. They introduced their motherland's paper-making and cloth-dyeing techniques to Japan. Some of these techniques still remain in the handcrafts of Mino's more isolated mountain regions.

Potters of Korean lineage built the split bamboo type kiln at Jōrin-ji, so far the only such kiln excavated in the Mino region. In order to construct such a large kiln and fire it, between ten and twenty people would have been required. Furthermore, they would have needed a wealthy and powerful patron as well as the cooperation of the people in the area.

Chinese ceramic culture spread to Japan in the form of imported pots. In contrast, Korean ceramic culture spread through direct interaction between human beings and became part of the Japanese artistic heritage by virtue of the fact that the Korean potters themselves became Japanese.

SEN NO RIKYŪ AND SETOGURO

When considering the development of Kiseto and Setoguro, one cannot forget the tea master Sen no Rikyū.

The concept that runs through the *wabi* tea ceremony is that of letting nature take its course, and Rikyū selected tea utensils for the quiet ease with which they entered the heart. In teabowls, his taste ran to black or brown monochrome, without decoration. However, the teabowls that the tea master Furuta Oribe selected, with their distorted, vigorous shapes, showed a completely different feeling. Sensual and dynamic, they were a frank expression of human emotion, and they stood in marked contrast to Rikyū's taste.

Rikyū was known to have favored two particular Kiseto flower vases. One is hour-glass shaped; the other is cylindrical, in the shape known as *tabi makura,* "traveler's pillow." On the inside of the cover of the wooden box containing the latter, an early Edo period man named Yamamoto Taian wrote: "The finest Kiseto hanging flower vase, prized by Rikyū. . . . " And the piece is without doubt worthy of Rikyū's *wabi* style of tea. Also, a lion-dog Kiseto incense burner owned by the Nezu Art Museum is supposed to have been highly treasured by Rikyū.

The teabowl *Oharagi* ("Ohara Wood"—Plates 41, 42), a fine example of Setoguro ware, was also owned by Rikyū. The inscription on the inside of the lacquered box lid, which reads *Oharagi,* has traditionally been attributed to Rikyū. The peerless Kiseto *wabi* teabowl known as *Asaina* has been passed down through generations in the Sen family. This teabowl, and the Setoguro *Oharame* ("Ohara Maiden") teabowl are practically identical in height, diameter, and shape and size of the foot. The two bowls were made in almost exactly the same way: the feet are extremely short; the inside of each foot has been trimmed with a wooden tool; the base outside each foot ring is broad; and the sides spring directly up from the base through the body.

Though the glazes are different, these two teabowls, representative of Kiseto and Setoguro ware, are otherwise the same in shape and construction.

They have both been handed down from very early on through the Sen family.

In the *Tsuda Sokyū chanoyu nikki* ("The Tea Ceremony Diary of Tsuda Sokyū"), dated 1572, a Seto teabowl was written about for the first time. Though what kind of teabowl it was is unknown, it is probably safe to say it was not a *tenmoku* bowl.

Taking all this into account, one may assume that, given their profound link to Rikyū's taste, the Mino pottery and the Kiseto and Setoguro flower vases and teabowls selected by Rikyū and other tea masters were fired and used in the same general time period.

In the *Sōtan nikki* ("Sōtan's Diary") of Kamiya Sōtan (1551–1635), it is recorded that Rikyū invited Sōtan and others to the Juraku palace on the 10th day of the 9th month of 1590 and there performed a tea ceremony for them. In the diary entry, Sōtan quotes Rikyū as saying: "I made tea in a black bowl, but since his lordship [Toyotomi Hideyoshi] disliked the bowl, I served him tea in this one [the one he was using in the tea ceremony with Sōtan]." In other words, this tells how when Rikyū had served Hideyoshi tea, he had at first used a black teabowl, but since Hideyoshi had disliked the bowl, Rikyū changed to a Seto teabowl.

In *Rikyū hyakkaiki* ("Journal of One Hundred Rikyū Tea Ceremonies"), compiled by Rikyū's disciples, there is the following entry for the 13th day of the 1st month of 1591: "I served tea in the Juraku two-mat room to his lordship [Hideyoshi], Maeda Toshiie, and Yakuin. I used a *kiri* kettle, a *wage* water jar, a black teabowl. . . ." Even though Rikyū knew that Hideyoshi disliked black teabowls, he dared to use one. This occurred just before Rikyū was ordered to commit ritual suicide, on the 28th day of the 2nd month of the same year.

Here we see Hideyoshi, who despised black teabowls and black seals (as opposed to red ones), because the latter were used on the birth registers of the lower classes, which reminded him of his humble birth, and Rikyū, who established black in his personal aesthetic. It tells graphically of the rivalry, brought out through tea, between Hideyoshi, the man of action who spurned matters intellectual, and Rikyū, who was ever in pursuit of a philosophical understanding of human nature.

During Hideyoshi's invasions of Korea, no one spoke out against the venture. In any case, Rikyū muttered a single protest: "This Asia campaign will be no more successful than trying to fight True Wisdom. . . ." These words were to cost him his life, as Yaeko Nogami shows in her book *Hideyoshi and Rikyū*, which brilliantly explores the riddle of Rikyū's last days.

Black is the one color that contains all other colors. Black is the one color that produces all other colors. Rikyū traded his life for that black teabowl. In the shadows of Momoyama period Setoguro pottery, which reach to our day, such human histories lie hidden.

SETOGURO TEABOWL SHAPES

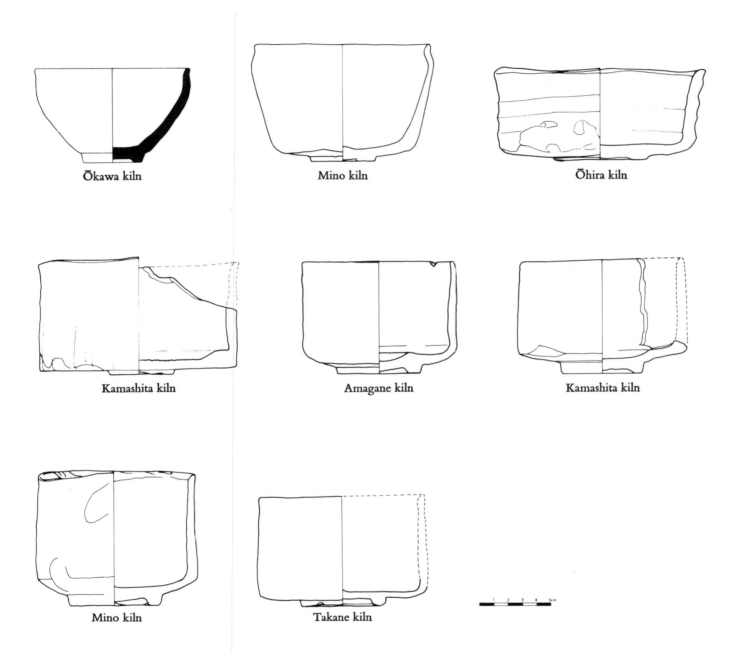

Ōkawa kiln

Mino kiln

Ōhira kiln

Kamashita kiln

Amagane kiln

Kamashita kiln

Mino kiln

Takane kiln

Mino Kiln Sites

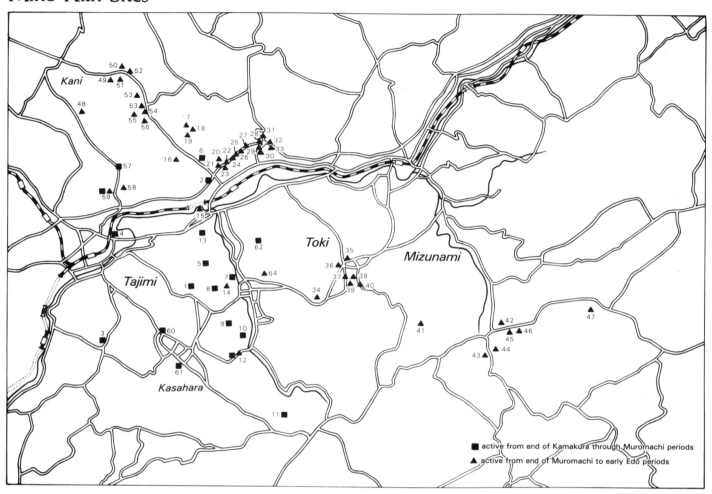

active from end of Kamakura through Muromachi periods

active from end of Muromachi to early Edo periods

1. Ōniba	33. Jōrinji Higashi No. 3 kiln site
2. Maruishi Higashi	34. Fujitsuka
3. Ichinokura	35. Kitayama
4. Kokeizan Maeyama	36. Nishiyama
5. Anakōbō	37. Taira
6. Hinata	38. Inokuchi
7. Nishiyama	39. Ariko
8. Kamabora	40. Higashikama
9. Kamane	41. Gōnoki
10. Guminoki	42. Tanoso
11. Ōgute	43. Ōkawa Nishi
12. Kamashita (Tsumaki)	44. Ōkawa Higashi
13. Tōshirō	45. Mizukami Nishi
14. Kamabata	46. Mizukami Higashi
15. Fukasawa	47. Mashizume Kamagahora
16. Hachiman	48. Sengen
17. Takane Nishi	49. Kamashita (Ōgaya)
18. Takane Kamasawa	50. Yashichida
19. Takane Higashi	51. Mutabora
20. Akasaba	52. Iwagahora
21. Kamagane (Kujiri)	53. Naka
22. Seianji	54. Yoshiemon
23. Motoyashiki	55. Seidayū
24. Inkyoyama Omote	56. Yamanokami
25. Inkyoyama Ura	57. Amagane
26. Ōtomi Nishi	58. Kamagane (Onada)
27. Ōtomi Higashi	59. Hakusan
28. Jōrinji Nishi No. 1 kiln site	60. Myōdo
29. Jōrinji Nishi No. 2 kiln site	61. Suegaoka
30. Jōrinji Nishi No. 3 kiln site	62. Higashiyama
31. Jōrinji Higashi No. 1 kiln site	63. Wakabayashi
32. Jōrinji Higashi No. 2 kiln site	64. Kamagane

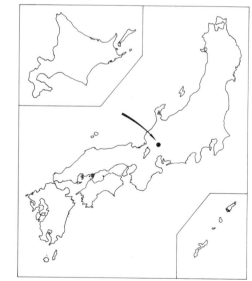

1

2

1, 2. Kiseto, flat bowl. D. 30.0 cm.

17

3

3. Kiseto, large rinka bowl, flower design. D. 25.2 cm. Fujita Art Museum.

4. Kiseto, large rinka bowl, radish design. D. 24.8 cm.

5

5. Kiseto bowl, plum branch design. D. 16.2 cm. MOA Museum of Art.

6. Kiseto bowl, cherry blossom design. D. 14.5 cm.

7. Kiseto, small serving dishes, cherry blossom design. D. 11.4–12.5 cm. Nezu Art Museum.

8. Kiseto, small serving dishes. D. 14.8 cm. Fujita Art Museum.

6

7

8

9

10

9–11. Kiseto, serving dishes, designs of grasses and flowers, five-piece service. D. 14.5–15.5 cm. Hatakeyama Collection.

11

12

13

14

12. *Kiseto water jar. H. 21.4 cm.*

13. *Kiseto, rinka saké cup. D. 8.0 cm., H. 6.4 cm.*

14. *Kiseto saké cup. D. 7.0 cm., H. 5.0 cm.*

15. *Kiseto round incense case. D. 6.5 cm.*

16. *Kiseto incense box in the shape of the Jewel of the Buddhist Law. H. 4.8 cm. Nezu Art Museum.*

17. *Kiseto incense burner. D. 7.3 cm., H. 5.9 cm.*

18. *Kiseto incense burner. D. 8.0 cm., H. 5.5 cm.*

19. *Kiseto incense burner. D. 7.3 cm., H. 6.0 cm.*

20. *Kiseto incense burner in the shape of a lion. H. 8.8 cm.*

21. *Kiseto incense burner in the shape of a lion. H. 10.0 cm. Umezawa Memorial Gallery.*

15

16

17

18

19

20

21

22

23

22, 23. Kiseto teabowl, dōjime type. D. 10.7 cm.
Hatakeyama Collection.

24

26

25

27

24, 25. Kiseto teabowl, low cylinder type. D. 9.2 cm.

26, 27. Kiseto teabowl, dōhimo type. D. 12.3 cm.

28

31

29

32

30

28

28–30. Setoguro teabowl. D. 14.6 cm. Box lid inscription.

31, 32. Setoguro teabowl. D. 12.4 cm.

33

34

35

36

33, 34. Setoguro saké cup. D. 7.2 cm., H. 6.2 cm.

35, 36. Setoguro teabowl. D. 13.0 cm.

37

37, 38. Setoguro teabowl; name: Himatsu *("Sun-lit Pine"). D. and H. 11.0 cm.*

38

30

39

39, 40. Setoguro teabowl; name: Fuyu no Yoru
("Winter Night"). D. and H. 10.0 cm.

40

41

43

42

41, 42. *Setoguro teabowl; name:* Oharagi *("Ohara Wood"). D. 10.2 cm., H. 8.8 cm.*

43–45. *Setoguro teabowl and box inscription. D. 13.7 cm.*

46, 47. *Setoguro teabowl. D. 15.4 cm.*

48, 49. *Setoguro teabowl; name:* Zazen *("Zen Meditation"). D. 16.0 cm.*

44

45

46

47

48

49

33

50a–d. Setoguro shards from the Kamashita kiln at Ōgaya.

51a–c. Setoguro shards from the Sengen kiln.

52a,b. Setoguro shards from the Ōhira kiln.

53a–d. Kiseto shards from the Sengen kiln.
54a–c. Kiseto shards from the Ōhira kiln.
55a–e. Kiseto shards from the Ōkawa kiln.
56a–c. Kiseto shards from the Naka kiln.

53b
53c
53d

54a
54b
54c

55a
55b
55c
55d
55e

56a
56b
56c

57

58

57. *Kiseto, large bowl, by Jūemon Katō. D. 27.8 cm. Kani Museum of Local History.*

58. *Setoguro teabowl, by Tōkurō Katō. D. 10.5–13.5 cm.*

Plate Notes

KISETO

Toward the end of the Muromachi period, when a large, partially above-ground kiln was built at Mino, somber, yellow Old Seto (Koseto) gave way to lighthearted Kiseto, and the black of *tenmoku* gave way to white Shino, in the deliberate experimentation with pottery that took place there. Against the backdrop of a free-spirited new age, these potters cast off the techniques they had learned from China and began to produce pottery congenial to the Japanese people. Kiseto is a pottery of ethereal beauty. As a pottery style, it quickly vanished after having left behind some excellent pieces made during the brief span of the Tenshō (1573–92) and Bunroku (1592–96) eras of the Momoyama period. A soft yellow glaze, fresh copper green, a mellow iron, a tranquil shape—these are the features of this Japanese beauty.

1, 2. Kiseto, flat bowl. D. 30.0 cm.

This bowl was excavated from the old kiln site at Ōkawa. Over its unique white ground, light yellow and fresh green glazes have been applied, and a simple wavy comb pattern along with a flower design have been incised. Although this is not a particularly famous piece, there are no other examples of such splendid workmanship, with its rough surface and the fireclay pad marks artlessly left behind. One can feel the fresh breeze of early Kiseto.

RINKA POTS

Rinka refers to a kind of vessel with a foliate rim. It is thought that such pottery forms were first an emulation of metalwork shapes. This technique can be seen in Heian period (794–1185) plates, in Kamakura period (1185–1333) ash-glazed incense burners with flower designs, and in iron-glazed Buddhist altar vases with floral scroll designs.

Momoyama period Kiseto moved completely away from the severity of the Chinese style, and the softer beauty of its *rinka* bowls, plates, serving dishes, saké cups, and so on, became a feature of Japanese pottery.

Subsequently, from the Momoyama period into the early Edo period, Kiseto *rinka* plates gradually gave way to Shino, *tenmoku*, and Mino Ofuke ware "chrysanthemum plates." These "chrysanthemum plates" were the last of Kiseto ware to die out, but by the middle of the Edo period they had almost completely disappeared.

Rinka vessels seem to speak softly of the Japanese taste and of one aspect of Japanese pottery.

3. Kiseto, large rinka bowl, flower design. D. 25.2 cm. Fujita Art Museum.

4. Kiseto, large rinka bowl, radish design. D. 24.8 cm.

Both of these bowls are fine examples of *rinka* pieces made in the Momoyama period.

Into the bowl in Plate 4, a radish has been incised with remarkably free and easy lines, and a faint copper green has permeated the pot's surface. One cannot but admire the skill of that unnamed potter, who could infuse an extremely commonplace vegetable with such refinement. The foliate rim is shaped with great ease. It is infused with such fragility that one wonders if it might not shatter when picked up.

In the bowl of Plate 3, lively stems radiate outward from the incised flower petals, creating a balanced design.

5. Kiseto bowl, plum branch design. D. 16.2 cm. MOA Museum of Art.

6. Kiseto bowl, cherry blossom design. D. 14.5 cm.

Various flower designs—irises, chrysanthemums, paulownia, flowering plants, cherry blossoms—decorate Kiseto pottery, but the plum blossom is used most frequently. In the bowl in Plate 5, an orderly branch of plum is depicted, and the effect is one of tidiness.

In the bottom of the bowl in Plate 6, a comb pattern is enclosed by concentric circles. Copper-green and iron underglazes are scattered in a lively manner, leaving an impression of mysterious brilliance. Although it may be hard to see in the photograph, both bowls have faint lattice patterns around their rims.

KISETO TABLEWARE OF THE MOMOYAMA PERIOD

In records of tea ceremonies, things used in a particular ceremony are minutely described, from teabowls, tea caddies, and water containers to the hanging scrolls and the food served. But there is hardly a mention of the plates on which the food was served.

While Sen no Rikyū declared that the tea ceremony was nothing more than boiling water and drinking tea, he was very fastidious about using only teabowls that satisfied the spirit. Surely he must have been just as particular about the vessels on which food was served. In fact, among Rikyū's possessions, and among the vessels handed down in the Sen family, there are many Kiseto pieces. The thought of what the five eye-catching dishes shown in Plates 9–11 would look like set out for meal service makes one's heart leap.

Amidst the changes in eating habits brought about by Japan's first contact with Europeans, and in the short time before the proliferation of Oribe tableware, Kiseto pieces must have complemented the flavors of the *kaiseki* meal, the light, elegant meal that is part of the tea ceremony.

7. Kiseto, small serving dishes, cherry blossom design. D. 11.4–12.5 cm. Nezu Art Museum.

These dishes show a *rinka* shape, created by notching each of the four sides from the base to the lip, although one of the dishes has, in fact, but the faintest of indentations, and then only on the lip. In the inside bottom of three of the dishes are marks from the round fireclay pads used to separate these dishes from the vessels set on top of them during firing. The cherry blossom designs were made with a flower stamp, and copper and iron were applied to the impressions.

These dishes were all probably made at the same time and at the same place, but each is slightly different from the others, and herein lies the interest of handmade wares.

Their fired surface resembles that of fired bean curd, and they are representative of the so-called "fried bean curd type" of Kiseto ware.

8. Kiseto, small serving dishes. D. 14.8 cm. Fujita Art Museum.
Rich copper green has been applied with an artless touch around the rims of this set of five serving dishes. Compared with modern articles, there is nothing monotonous about these five pieces. When lined up, they are distinctively set off from each other by their free, almost whimsical, hand-painted patterns.

9–11. Kiseto, serving dishes, designs of grasses and flowers, five-piece service. D. 14.5–15.5 cm. Hatakeyama Collection.

Four sides of each of these shallow serving dishes have been pinched to form a *rinka* shape, and a different picture is seen on each plate. The surface of each of the plates is a perfect "fried bean curd" texture, and a refreshing copper green has been boldly applied. The various grass and flower designs have been incised with the straightforward use of a pointed tool, resulting in a diversity of composition among the five dishes. These are superior examples of Kiseto serving dishes.

12. Kiseto water jar. H. 21.4 cm.
This is most unusual for a Kiseto water jar. Its unique shape seems inspired by the pantaloons depicted in contemporary paintings of Europeans. The lip is elevated, and the shoulder and body of the pot were thrown on the wheel. After this, the feet were formed by pushing in the clay. The size and

placement of the ears serve to tighten the composition of the piece.

13. Kiseto, rinka saké cup. D. 8.0 cm., H. 6.4 cm.
This is a beautifully shaped *rinka* piece, of the type that might be used in a formal Japanese place setting. The glaze effect is superior, and the copper green adds a bright elegance.

14. Kiseto saké cup. D. 7.0 cm., H. 5.0 cm.
This piece shows the glazing style known as "saké cup type" (*guinomi-de*). The cup was first thrown on a wheel, then taken off and molded into a hexagonal shape. There must have been many saké cups made in this manner.

In the inside bottom of the cup glaze has accumulated, which is ideal for a saké cup.

KISETO INCENSE BURNERS AND BOXES

15. Kiseto round incense box. D. 6.5 cm.

16. Kiseto incense box in the shape of the Jewel of the Buddhist Law. H. 4.8 cm. Nezu Art Museum.

17. Kiseto incense burner. D. 7.3 cm., H. 5.9 cm.

18. Kiseto incense burner. D. 8.0 cm., H. 5.5 cm.

19. Kiseto incense burner. D. 7.3 cm., H. 6.0 cm.

20. Kiseto incense burner in the shape of a lion. H. 8.8 cm.

21. Kiseto incense burner in the shape of a lion. H. 10.0 cm. Umezawa Memorial Gallery.

The work in Plate 16 is a masterpiece, easily considered the finest of Kiseto incense boxes. The entire surface, covered with the characteristic Kiseto glaze, shows a "fried bean curd" skin of the highest quality. The light and dark copper green at the top of the lid and the dots of black iron are of incomparable beauty.

In Plate 15, the faint iron color combines with tiny specks of copper to give a tidy appearance.

Plates 17–19 show small incense burners that call to mind sections of bamboo. Even from among these simple pots, a variety of effects emerges.

The pieces in Plates 20 and 21 are incense burners in the form of lions. The notches along the shoulder show the lions' mane, and those around the legs seem to represent shaggy fur. Yet at the same time they serve to strengthen the places where the different parts of the pot have been joined. These pieces have a very unusual design, with the powerful forelegs and slender hind legs giving the impression that the animal could pounce at any moment.

KISETO TEABOWLS

22, 23. Kiseto teabowl, dōjime type. D. 10.7 cm. Hatakeyama Collection.

This is a generously shaped, even plump bowl. Its lip, too, is soft. Its base is in the gently curved "go-stone box" shape often found in Kiseto works. And its form is pulled together by a single shelflike line, called a *dōjime*, which encircles the trunk.

The piece was probably originally intended as a serving dish, but its copper green and iron markings harmonize with its rather thin "fried bean curd" surface. It makes a beautiful teabowl.

This piece is supposed to have been made at the Kamashita kiln at Ōgaya, a site known for firing superior Kiseto ware.

24, 25. Kiseto teabowl, low cylinder type. D. 9.2 cm.
The *dōhimo* line encircling the bowl unusually close to the lip enlivens what might otherwise be a rather monotonous shape. The incised grass design with a forceful copper green applied to it also gives the piece vigor. The glaze melted incompletely, giving the effect usually found in saké cups, yet a soft, relaxed color is the result. In the inside of the foot is the mark left behind by a round fireclay pad. This piece was probably made as a cylindrical serving bowl, but came to be used as a teabowl, a use for which it is well suited.

26, 27. Kiseto teabowl, dōhimo *type. D. 12.3 cm.*
Soft color is the strong point of Kiseto ware. The lightly fired glaze and the freely incised scroll patterns are drawn together by the pinched *dōhimo* line that encircles the bow like a narrow belt. This was originally intended as a serving dish and lacks the accent of copper green. It is a fine piece of tableware. Inside the foot (Plate 27) one can see a faint red mark made by the round fireclay pad used to separate pieces when stacked in the kiln.

28–30. Setoguro teabowl. D. 14.6 cm. Box lid inscription.
One can tell at a glance that this is a splendid early Setoguro teabowl. The three powerful raised lines made on the wheel, the stable shape, the low foot with wide ring. . . . The fingermarks left on the artless glazing go well with the strong lip and tell us a great deal about the Momoyama spirit. The inscription on the box is by Toyozō Arakawa the contemporary "Living National Treasure."

31, 32. Setoguro teabowl. D. 12.4 cm.
This is a rare teabowl, showing the form that early Setoguro took. The lip is that of a *tenmoku* teabowl, but the body is well rounded down through the base, and the low and wide foot ring was designed for added stability when removing the piece from the kiln during firing. As is clearly visible in the photograph, a vivid mark has been left by the tongs used to pull the piece from the kiln, and this adds to the effect. One can read a lot in this bowl about the evolution from *tenmoku* to Setoguro teabowls.

33, 34. Setoguro saké cup. D. 7.2 cm., H. 6.2 cm.
This cup was excavated from the Sengen kiln and is an unusual example of a small Setoguro bowl. It was thrown on a wheel and is completely covered with glaze. The way it is made reminds one of Black Raku, and I can imagine

that there was some exchange of techniques between Kiseto and Raku potters. Was this piece designed to test some process at the Sengen kiln, where a great number of Setoguro teabowls were made? This bowl is a masterpiece, and undoubtedly much favored for drinking saké.

35, 36. Setoguro teabowl. D. 13.0 cm.
Though this piece was not fired as thoroughly as most Setoguro teabowls, it nonetheless shows a jet-black luster. Judging from the marks left when it was removed from the kiln, the glaze used seems to have been designed for low temperatures. The inside of the foot was left unglazed, allowing a glimpse of the clay. Everything else, including the foot ring, has been glazed—a technique similar to that used in Raku ware. But while Raku bowls are hand built, this bowl was thrown on a wheel, using a vertically held tool, and its foot is sharply delineated. It is probably a piece made in Mino by a potter who had some background in Raku.

37, 38. Setoguro teabowl; name: Himatsu *("Sunlit Pine"). D. 11.0 cm., H. 11.0 cm.*
This pot has a thick, round rim. The throwing marks are exaggerated, and the body has been firmly pressed in above the base. The small foot, and the marked trimming on the base are rare compared to the low, horizontal bases usually found on Setoguro bowls. The glaze has been naturally, artlessly, applied, as though by someone who had turned to making a teabowl after having churned out kiln saggars for some time. The white marks around the base, which were by the potter's fingers, and the diagonal tong marks notched into the body, are vivid evidence of this bowl's visit to the kiln.

39, 40. Setoguro teabowl; name: Fuyu no Yoru *("Winter Night"). D. 10.0 cm., H. 10.0 cm.*
There is hardly anything mannered about this whole piece. The fact that a vertically held tool was lightly used when throwing the body is all but unnoticeable. The lip, too, comes to a gentle peak, and the body grows outward down through the hip. The foot is not so low and has been trimmed all around.

The black glaze is iridescent. This piece is renowned as a Setoguro teabowl of great charm.

41, 42. Setoguro teabowl; name: Oharagi *("Ohara Wood"). D. 10.2 cm., H. 8.8 cm.*
Vertical tool marks run down the body from lip to base, and as if to pull them together, the lip comes to a thick, soft peak. With this, and the lip's powerful curve, the work is rather like a Black Oribe bowl. The low, small foot has been effortlessly trimmed with a wooden tool. The large glazeless triangle on the bottom of the body contrasts splendidly with the jet-black glaze. This bowl was probably made when Setoguro ware was at its full maturity.

This piece was owned by Sen no Rikyū, and the *Oharagi* inscription on its box is attributed to him. It is a famous example of Setoguro.

43–45. Setoguro teabowl. Box lid inscription. D. 13.7 cm.
This piece looks as though it just came into being naturally, without the aid of human hands. It is from the Sengen kiln. The inscription, by Toyozō Arakawa, reads: "This was excavated from the old Sengen mountain kiln site, in Kukuri, Mino. It must be from the Momoyama period."

The yellowish-brown color of this piece (instead of the usual jet black) probably comes from its being left to cool slowly in the kiln after firing.

46, 47. Setoguro teabowl. D. 15.4 cm.
This bowl must have been made during the prime of Setoguro's short life. Both the superb glaze and the solid shape make this a fine example of a large Setoguro teabowl. One senses from this bowl that its potter still had talent to spare.

48, 49. Setoguro teabowl; name: Zazen ("Zen Meditation"). D. 16.0 cm.
There is probably no other piece of pottery with such splendid depth of jet-black glaze, such marvelous black color. The mark left on the surface facing the fire contributes to the overall effect and leaves an even more profound impression. The bold form of the piece calls to mind a solitary monk sunk deep in contemplation in the meditation hall of a temple.

When one comes close to this bowl, it is as though one could be overwhelmed by some unnamed power.

50a–d. Setoguro shards from the Kamashita kiln at Ōgaya.
51a–c. Setoguro shards from the Sengen kiln.
52a, b. Setoguro shards from the Ōhira kiln.
53a–d. Kiseto shards from the Sengen kiln.
54a–c. Kiseto shards from the Ōhira kiln.
55a–e. Kiseto shards from the Ōkawa kiln.
56a–c. Kiseto shards from the Naka kiln.
In Plates 50–56, Kiseto and Setoguro shards from the major kilns are arranged by kiln site. These shards provide corroborating evidence for proving that a particular piece is from a particular kiln. Furthermore, though they are only fragments, one can still take pleasure in their superb workmanship.

The Kamashita kiln at Ōgaya is well known for the superior Kiseto ware it produced. The pieces counted as the finest of Kiseto are thought, for the most part, to have come from this kiln. However, since many Kiseto shards from Kamashita were destroyed in the war, none could be shown here. Sometime I hope to run across some Kiseto shards from this famous kiln and learn more about it.

The Ōhira kilns were famous for their Shino ware, but they do not have much of a reputation for Kiseto. However, judging from the beauty of the glazing and copper-green markings shown here, there is no doubt that some fine Kiseto was fired at this kiln site.

Furthermore, although complete Setoguro teabowls from the Sengen and Kamashita kilns are few, quite a few teabowl fragments have been excavated at these sites. In order to produce a few superb pieces, naturally a huge quantity of test pieces ended up on the waste pile. That the hidden story of these shards cannot be learned simply gives dimension and life to the few famous complete pots.

MODERN KISETO AND SETOGURO

As is explained in detail in the text, the production of Kiseto and Setoguro ware reached its peak briefly in the Momoyama period then quickly died out.

But through the efforts of a number of potters, there has been a revival in the making of these two types of pottery, along with Shino and Oribe ware, beginning in the 1920s. However, the changes wrought by our modern life-style, and our destruction of the environment, have had a profound impact on pottery. In the case of Kiseto, for example, the warm feeling of the color found in the Momoyama pieces owes a great deal to wood ash. Today it has become all but impossible to obtain the hardwood needed to produce the ash most suitable for Kiseto. Further, kilns are no longer fired with wood or charcoal, but, rather with gas, oil, and electricity. But even under these circumstances, zealous study of Kiseto and Setoguro goes on today.

Plate 57 shows a bowl made by the late Jūemon Katō of Gifu Prefecture, who was designated an "Intangible Cultural Property." Though the bowl follows traditional Kiseto techniques, there is an air of the modern about it that one cannot quite isolate.

Plate 58 shows a Setoguro teabowl by Tōkurō Katō. He puts scrupulous care into his work, following the aphorism: "Be sensitive when making small pieces; think 'vigor' when making large ones." Because Tōkurō thinks in these terms, he has come quite close to the Momoyama ideal in his endeavors in Kiseto, Setoguro, Shino, and Oribe. And one can see him walking where no one has walked before, going beyond Shigaraki, Iga, and Karatsu ware, to open new worlds of pottery.

57. Kiseto, large bowl, by Jūemon Katō. D. 27.8 cm. Kani Museum of Local History.
58. Setoguro teabowl, by Tōkurō Katō. D. 10.5–13.5 cm.

定価3,500円
in Japan